Table of Contents

GET ONLINE

CHAPTER 1

Why speed is important and size doesn't matter

CHAPTER 2

It's not who you know, it's who knows you

GROW ONLINE

CHAPTER 3

Redefining borders in an ever-expanding market

CHAPTER 4

Finding your voice in the worldwide conversation

CHAPTER 5

How small brands stand out in a crowd

THRIVE ONLINE

the small think big book

How today's small businesses are using the web to win

By Arjan Dijk
& Sandeep Menon

Foreword

The Internet has always been a great leveler, democratizer, and anonymizer for individuals. One of the most iconic *New Yorker* cartoons from the late 1990s featured a dog in front of a computer screen with the caption, "On the Internet, no one knows you're a dog."

Today, the same could be said about businesses: On the Internet, no one knows you're a small business. The emergence of tools and services that make it simple and inexpensive to establish a meaningful web presence and drive a business forward has been one of the most important developments of the last decade. Now any business — of any size — can look and feel like a Fortune 500 company and build its brand and customer base without spending a fortune.

The Small Think Big Book: How Today's Small Businesses Are Using the Web to Win captures the essence of these trends in a very accessible format. Full of rich examples from Arjan and Sandeep's many years of experience working with small business clients at Google, this book is the perfect primer for the 75 percent of small businesses and startups around the world that still don't have a web presence, and for the 25 percent that do — but could stand to improve it.

Small businesses aren't the only ones who can benefit from the important insights in this book. With the proliferation of online marketing tools and channels, and the dizzying pace of technical innovation, marketers of larger companies will find many valuable lessons here to help them face the challenges of the digital age.

Since joining the Direct Marketing Association's Board of Directors four years ago, I have worked closely with Arjan to advance the cause of responsible data-driven marketing. *The Small Think Big Book* is a great back-to-basics reminder for all of us about the essentials of building a brand and an audience that marries the fundamentals of marketing to the most widely accessible Internet data, tools, and techniques available today.

Matt Blumberg
Chairman & CEO, Return Path, Inc.
Chairman, Direct Marketing Association
New York, NY

Introduction
Welcome to the infinite market

F ive or so years ago, when we first started working together at Google, there was still a widely held belief among many in the marketing field that big companies held most of the cards when it came to growth, innovation, and economic success. Armed with big budgets for advertising, marketing, and research, large corporations believed they could spread their reach much further and absorb costly missteps. Small businesses, on the other hand, were generally perceived as limited in scope and slow to adapt — stuck in a brick-and-mortar world of Yellow Pages, billboards, and newspaper circulars. Big companies thought in terms of millions, small businesses in terms of dozens.

Having spent many years at multinational corporations (Capital One, Unilever, SAP, Citibank) in analytics and brand marketing, we didn't believe that to be the case anymore. We were convinced that given the right tools, training, and opportunity, small businesses could not only succeed online, they could compete on the same playing field with businesses 10 or 100 times their size.

Google tasked us with taking a structured, programmatic approach to the way we looked at small businesses, and sure enough, within a few months, the numbers started proving our approach was right. We saw that with even a modest effort, small businesses that harnessed the power of the Internet could achieve astronomic growth rates. According to Google research,[1] in 2010, businesses with a high web presence reported nearly double the sales volume of businesses without any web presence at all.

The problem we came to see, however, was a disconnect between the number of small businesses starting up every year and the number that embraced the web to grow and thrive.

Despite the fact that small firms and start-ups account for nearly two-thirds of present-day job growth in the United States (with medium-sized companies making up the other third),[2] upwards of 58 percent of them don't have a website. When you consider that an overwhelming majority of American consumers today look online for local products and services, the importance of bridging that gap becomes abundantly clear.

Our goal with this book is to show you how small business can compete with big business in the digital marketplace by using free and low-cost tools to target, acquire, and retain customers, and analyze performance data to improve their bottom line. We believe that in today's world, you no longer need a high-profile New York creative agency, a research division, or a PhD in computer science to run an effective marketing operation. You simply need to meet your customers where they are.

To that end, we've divided the book into three sections. The first section, Get Online, goes over some basics that many of you will already be familiar with but that can serve as a primer for those just getting started in the online world. Here, we cover the importance of speed over size, how to establish a web presence, and how to make sure you're found online.

The second section, Grow Online, offers a number of approaches for leveling the playing field, both at home and abroad. From using the web to become a local hero, to taking a local company global and harnessing the power of social media to market your business — we offer numerous practical tips and examples to show you what can be done.

The third section, Thrive Online, addresses the biggest stumbling blocks — and in many ways the biggest opportunities — for small businesses in the digital marketplace: Differentiating yourself from the competition, tracking performance, analyzing data, and understanding both your customers and your channels. Our aim is to dispel some myths and remove the fear factor around what we call data-driven "nerdy marketing."

If you've spent any time in the business world, you've likely heard the old adage: I know that half of my advertising dollars are wasted … I just don't know which half. By the time you've finished this book, we hope you'll have a clear understanding of how to get your business online, how to market it effectively using simple and inexpensive tools and data, and how to maximize your revenue without wasting your advertising dollars.

A QUICK NOTE:

As you read this book, you'll notice we talk a lot about Google products. While we realize there are other products out there, we work at Google, we know Google products, we really like Google products, and we support Google products. However, this does not mean we are pushing Google products above all others or that our suggestions constitute the final word on the subject. As in all endeavors, it pays to do your homework and figure out what works best for you.

CHAPTER 1

Fast Beats Big
Why speed is important and size doesn't matter

L et's imagine that you're reading this book on a Nexus 7 tablet. If you are the proud owner of a first-generation tablet, you might notice a few things right now. Not only is the picture sharper and the color more vibrant, but this little machine has serious horsepower. In fact, it's many times faster than any of its predecessors — about the same speed as the fastest supercomputer was some 20 years ago.

While you consider the fact that this remarkable development was accomplished in less time than it takes to get a college degree, also consider that your kids already think the Nexus 7 tablet is *sooo* last month and are scouring the web to see when the next version is coming out.

A 2011 survey[3] found that 30 percent of U.S. children between the ages of three and five use the web daily, and that 67 percent are online regularly by age eight. Another recent study[4] estimated that more than 90 percent of American children under the age of two already have an online history.

"We are living in exponential times," says technology chronicler Karl Fisch in his YouTube video, "Did You Know?" which catalogs mind-boggling facts about globalization and the information age. Fisch and others note some of the astounding technological milestones we've already reached and ones we will reach in the next few years, among them:

- Between 2008 and 2012, 902 million people worldwide went online, bringing the global Internet user total to 2.4 billion. In the United States alone, 78 percent of the population uses the Internet.[5]

- In 1984, there were 1,000 Internet devices. In 1992, there were one million. In 2008, there were one billion.

- By 2016, the number of mobile-connected devices will exceed the number of people on earth (7.3 billion).[6]

- There are 100 billion searches on Google every month. In 2006, that number was just 2.7 billion.[7]

- It took 38 years for radio to reach a market audience of 50 million. It took the Internet just four years to reach it.

Our point is not to make your head spin or to suggest that your kids are light-years ahead of you in their ability to adapt to the pace of change. (Let's face it, they are.) It's to show you how a rapidly changing digital landscape might tilt the scales in your favor.

Today, more than ever before, the pace — and price — of technological innovation is leveling the playing field for small businesses. Tools and technologies that were once unattainably expensive are now available to all for minimal or even no cost.

The rise in global Internet access for both consumers and business owners, combined with its ability to reach millions in minutes and address market shifts in days or weeks (versus months or years), is democratizing the marketplace.

Big companies may have the resources and budgets to conduct large-scale research, establish systems and processes, and hire fancy agencies to run their advertising campaigns, but those systems and processes by their very nature are resistant to change. The bigger the ship, the slower it turns.

Unencumbered by expensive, entrenched, and outmoded systems, unimpeded by layers of management bureaucracy that bog down decision making, small to medium-sized businesses (SMBs) can use agility to their advantage.

Speed, in other words, is your friend.

But where do you begin? For those used to doing business the old-fashioned way, one customer at a time, the choices may seem overwhelming. Just when you thought a simple website would do, you're barraged with a thousand other options — cloud technology, mobile optimization, social networking — and on and on.

One way to approach it is to look at a few businesses that started small and used the flexibility and speed of online tools and marketing to compete and succeed against bigger companies.

Coolhaus is a made-to-order ice-cream sandwich company that began as a single truck in Los Angeles. Cofounders Natasha Case and Freya Estreller took their passion for architecture and design and used it to reinvent this frozen American classic. (Coolhaus takes its name from the haus in Bauhaus design and Dutch architect Rem Koolhaas.) The pair focused on market-fresh and eco-friendly ingredients, incorporating these principles into every aspect of the business, down to edible wrappers.

With a personal credit card and $700 borrowed from a friend, they bought an old postal truck and towed it to the Coachella Valley Music Festival in 2009. Doing tent-to-tent marketing and posting updates and photos on Twitter, Estreller and Case introduced festivalgoers to "farchitecture" — food architecture — offering unusual flavor combos, such as oatmeal cookies stacked with cinnamon ice cream.

After the festival, the website Curbed did a small write-up, and within 48 hours, Case says, "We had 2,000 Twitter followers … Pretty soon, people were calling to get our truck at film sets, office events, birthday parties. *Los Angeles* magazine got wind of it. And we hadn't even retrofitted the truck yet."

At a large company, where systems and processes need to be in place, staff needs to be hired, and office space needs to be rented before launch, putting the cart before the horse might have been a serious problem, says Case. But Coolhaus benefited from creating community and building buzz before it had established itself fully as a business.

"In today's online culture, people can know about a brand or a product long before you actually launch. That's a huge difference from before," she says. "Restaurants, for instance, can do a pop-up at an established place and let people try their food before they open an actual restaurant. They can try out their menus, refine their concept, and then use data from these events to get a feel for what people are asking for."

By the beginning of 2011, using online tools such as Twitter and the review site Yelp, as well as its own website and blog, Coolhaus had both expanded its repertoire substantially and built a large enough following to launch a truck in New York.

"We started to talk about New York on our website and Twitter feed in 2010, so by the time we opened [less than a year later], there was a line around the block," remembers Case.

New York led to Austin and Miami, followed by a brick-and-mortar shop in Culver City, California, and distribution in 25 Whole Foods markets. Today, the company grosses nearly $3 million in annual sales.

In addition to leveraging low-cost high-speed technology, one of the biggest pluses of using online services and tools is the ability to track sales and manage customer relations. Coolhaus uses USA ePay, which allows it to track sales in real time so it can quickly see what's selling and what's not; Google Drive to initiate customer-satisfaction surveys and develop sales leads; and Google Calendar to publicize truck locations and special events.

"In the past, if you opened a shop in a neighborhood, you had to circulate flyers, pound the pavement. It took a lot longer to establish your customer base, and it cost a lot more," says Case. "Now, if we get a negative review, we write back immediately. We offer a coupon, a gift certificate; we ask the reviewer to give us a second chance. Customers are amazed and appreciative that the owners of the company are attending to them. Online allows you to make that connection."

The idea of testing a market or a product before launch used to be something only big companies with big budgets could do. For a large company, spending millions on the rollout of a new product only to have it fail was expensive but not necessarily devastating (remember New Coke?). For small businesses that couldn't afford these kinds of mistakes, however, it often came down to guesswork. "Spray and pray" — slapping flyers and billboards up all over town in the hopes that something would catch a consumer's eye and stick — was the primary method, and its effectiveness was dubious.

Today, a variety of Internet tools have made test-marketing a viable option for small businesses.

Take the example of Timothy Ferriss, author of *The 4-Hour Workweek: Escape 9–5, Live Anywhere, and Join the New Rich*. Given that some 200,000 books are published in the U.S. each year, Ferriss' book might have wallowed (like hundreds of others) at the bottom of the Amazon sales rankings. Instead, using simple, inexpensive technology, he was able to leapfrog his competition and rocket to the ranks of the *New York Times* bestseller list.

After finishing his early-retirement manifesto, Ferriss decided to test several different titles for the book to see which one consumers responded to best. Over the course of a week, he identified six strong contenders, then narrowed it down to three: *Broadband and White Sand*, *Millionaire Chameleon*, and *The 4-Hour Workweek*.

Next, he bought ads on Google Search and launched a campaign on AdWords, using keywords related to the book's content, such as 401(k) and language learning. Whenever those keywords formed part of someone's Google search, a title candidate would appear as the ad headline, and a short synopsis would form the advertisement text. Then, he tracked which of the ads was clicked on the most. At the end of the week (and for less than $200), he recognized *The 4-Hour Workweek* as the victor by a healthy margin.

By the time he published his book, Ferriss already had a title and cover that he knew were surefire hits. (He tested dust jackets by watching shoppers peruse the shelves at various bookstores.) From there, the clicks kept coming. To date, Ferriss has sold more than 1,350,000 copies.

Perhaps less sensational but nonetheless remarkable is the story of Dead Sea Cosmetics, a small company that combined speed, flexibility, and quick reflexes to turn an experiment into a successful online business. Created by a Czechoslovakian advertising agency to test the validity of search advertising for its clients, Dead Sea Cosmetics began as an online cosmetics shop with products sourced from the Dead Sea. It did so well, the shop quickly evolved into a full-scale e-business, with a complete line of more than 50 products. The key, according to company spokesman Peter Ladman, was allocating 100 percent of the budget to online communication and advertising.

"Even though we counted on [search ads] to increase conversions and sales, we were surprised how well they work," says Ladman. "AdWords is a flexible product and allows us to reach our target groups easily, from beauticians in their beauty shops to end-users in their homes.

Google AdWords is a way to advertise and market your product, service, or business in the Google search engine. Online text ads appear as "sponsored links" when people search for phrases related to your business. Advertisers bid for keyword phrases, but only pay when someone clicks on the ad as a result of a web search.

At one point, Ladman notes, mud from the Dead Sea was so popular, the shop couldn't keep up with demand and had to take it off the menu. A delayed shipment of silt at the border further compounded the shortage. But what would have been a setback 20 years ago instead became a springboard. The company was able to respond immediately, placing a temporary halt on both search and other online advertising for the mud products. Implementing the change was as easy as flipping a switch. "When the product finally arrived, we used search advertising to report to our customers that the goods were in stock again. Immediately after the announcement, there was a huge avalanche of new orders."

While fluctuations in the marketplace are nothing new, being able to quickly respond, shift gears, and ride short bursts of traffic as a result of changes in supply, popularity, or even a mistake is something small companies couldn't do before. Only in today's digital environment do SMBs have the tools to react and alter strategies with the click of a mouse.

For small businesses and start-ups, the speed of change means not just a level playing field and a chance to make it to the big leagues, but an opportunity to invent a whole new ball game.

CHAPTER 2

Where You Live Online
It's not who you know, it's who knows you

To become a successful business — online or offline — your customers first need to find you. Not that long ago, they found you because they walked past your business or because they lived nearby. The medium wasn't as important as convenience and proximity. But in today's infinite market, proximity is everywhere, and around the corner might as well be a million miles away when you can simply click a mouse or tap a tablet.

Consequently, how and where your customers find you has become as crucial as finding you in the first place.

Today, it's estimated that 97 percent of American consumers are searching for products online[8] — even those people who live right around the corner. Local customers don't need to walk to your business to figure out if you have what they want. And they will have done their homework before they knock on your door. Remember the old Yellow Pages line, "Let your fingers do the walking"? That logic still applies to customers in the Internet age: Avoid disappointment, and don't waste my time.

The ease and speed of web searching has also made customers nosier. They don't just want to know if you have their size or color, they want to know who else bought that shoe, what the quality and fit were like, and whether it's worth their time to check it out personally.

Undoubtedly, all these unsolicited opinions can be a double-edged sword, but wielded correctly, they mean your reputation will drive your reach.

Given that most of the world now looks online for products and services they used to seek out in person, it may surprise you to hear this statistic: Of the approximately 90 million active SMBs around the globe, only about 25 percent have a website.[9]

Even that doesn't tell the whole story. Among those that do have websites, many are rudimentary, bare-bones, and woefully inadequate. No address. No phone number. No call to action. Unreadable fonts. Unusable navigation. Broken links. The list goes on.

If you've ever clicked on a blinking neon banner ad only to be whisked away to an unreadable site that has absolutely nothing to do with the advertised product or service (Viagra anyone?), then you know what we're talking about.

Needless to say, websites are an essential — perhaps the most essential — first step for any small business trying to establish an online presence. A website lets you show (rather than tell) your customers about your business. Think about it this way: When was the last time you bought a book or went to a movie without first checking the reviews online? Or booked a hotel without viewing the rooms? Or searched for a hairdresser without checking the location?

In our opinion, a business without a website is like a superhero wearing a cloak of invisibility. Your business may indeed be super-powered, but you still need to give people a way to find you.

For those who have yet to take this first step, here's the good news: Launching a website is easy, cheap, and most importantly, rewarding. Recent research shows that SMBs that use web technology regularly grow twice as fast as those that don't.[10] In 2010, businesses with a high web presence reported nearly double the sales volume of businesses without any web presence.

There are many free — or nearly free — options out there to help you get set up. Most of these web hosting, designing, and managing services come complete with features that your customers already know and have come to expect — shopping carts, calendars, navigable maps, photo layouts, even transaction functions. Something as simple as a business listing on a map can go a long way to helping customers find you when they search for products in their local area.

If you're still feeling wary, here are a few more reasons to establish a web presence.

A website ensures you never turn anyone away
Having a website means your business is never closed, and you'll spend less time answering the phone, returning e-mails, and responding to questions you probably hear again and again. By providing basic information and answering frequently asked questions online, you'll ensure no one walks away disappointed.

A website expands your customer base
With a website, your potential customers are no longer limited to your neighborhood, your city, state, or even

your country. Customers can (and do) come from all over the world.

A website adds to your revenue stream

A website lets you supplement your brick-and-mortar business with additional online products, providing a low-overhead revenue stream. There may be products, programs, or specials you want to offer only online. In many cases, you don't even require a product in stock to identify the marketplace need. If you want to expand but don't have the capital, your website provides an excellent avenue for growth.

A website helps you understand customers' needs

A website allows you to change, tailor, and update your information as often as you like, as well as track customers' responses to maximize profits. Free online tools can show you who visits your site, what products or sections are most compelling, and what factors lead up to initial and repeat purchases.

A website is a direct line of communication to customers

The ability to converse and engage directly with customers and prospective customers is a key advantage in today's socially driven online world. A website can open up the lines of communication, establishing a one-on-one relationship that's not based on — or limited to — proximity.

Rafaela Parmejani, owner of Menina da Villa (Girl of the Villa), an urban spa in São Paulo, Brazil, makes a strong case for the value of a website. Before opening her spa, Parmejani relied on direct mail and word of mouth to attract local customers. "People were constantly asking if I had a website, and when I told them that I didn't, they were immediately turned off," she says.

Parmejani found a free online program to set up her site, and one of the first features she implemented was a scheduling tool. Almost immediately, people in her neighborhood — people who had never expressed interest in her spa before — started coming in. Within a few months, her customer inflow had increased 50 to 60 percent.

The lesson she learned was that even customers who lived nearby felt more comfortable doing business with her spa when they could browse her product offerings, get a feel for the atmosphere, and make appointments from home at their convenience, any time of day or night.

Consumers today want to make an informed decision, and a website gives them that power. Sumul Shah, president of Lumus Construction, a contractor specializing in historic restorations and renewable energy, found that a web presence was essential for defining the company's identity. As a builder who was often in the running for government contracts, his website doubled as a calling card.

Shah felt that a well-designed, highly visual website could act as a showcase for the company's past work and give potential clients a tangible way to decide if it was a good fit for their project.

"When we first started, we really needed to get images of our projects out to our customers. They just weren't connecting with our verbal descriptions," Shah explains. "The website was our best tool because it helped customers visualize both the types of projects and the complexity of work that we do."

Shah predicts that in the future, the company's website will be able to quantify renewable energy data by taking live data from its wind turbines and solar panels, assimilating the information, and reporting how much energy has been produced. With the data doing the heavy lifting to broadcast Lumus' environmental credentials, the company won't need to rely as much on word of mouth, and potential clients can use this wealth of information to guide their decisions.

Here's one more example that shows how even an old-world brick-and-mortar business can make a successful transition to online sales.

Lukasz Prokopowicz and his parents, Anna and Andrew, run a specialty gourmet butcher shop in Warsaw, Poland, selling sausage, natural meats, wine, and bakery goods. When they started out nearly 20 years ago, they relied almost entirely on local word of mouth for their advertising.

In 2009, Prokopowicz decided it was time to expand and go online. He found a simple program to create a website and started with the basics — a few photos, a description of what the shop offered, its name and address. From there, he added an online shop that showcased their products, setting up categories to steer customers quickly to what they wanted (meats, sauces, baked dishes, items for kids), as well as a search function to help people locate specific products.

Now he needed a way to help new customers who didn't live in the neighborhood find the store. So, he added a locator button for the shop on Google Maps and then turned to advertising to spread the word. Prokopowicz says he tried the local press first but soon found he had much more success online with Google AdWords.

"In simple words, I am [no longer] looking for customers by attacking them with invasive ads, but [customers] are finding my ad when they look for a specific product."

He began by choosing a few key search terms for his ads, so that when someone searched for types of meat in combination with words like shopping and home delivery, his store came up. He then defined what his campaign target was (an online purchase) and let AdWords do the rest.

After three months, Prokopowicz reports that he had brought more than 3,000 visitors to the website and online store. No doubt many more found the site online and made the trip to the brick-and-mortar shop, which in turn increased positive reviews and foot traffic. Today, the shop is known throughout Poland and in many other places around the world.

These are just a few examples of how something as simple as a website can have profound implications — for customers, for employees, and for a company's bottom line.

As you plan your first website or think about adding to it, we recommend looking for ways to let your web presence reflect your industry. What are the main reasons customers come to your site? What are their needs? What are the most important things you want them to know about your business?

Keep in mind, of course, that a web presence is not a magic bullet, it's just one part of the marketing matrix, the first step to tapping your online potential.

Once you're on the Internet, the sky's the limit.

CHAPTER 3

Local Goes Global
Redefining borders in an ever-expanding market

As a small company, the scope of your reputation is relative. You may consider your company a tiny speck on a national level, but in your hometown, it could be a celebrated household name. Using the worldwide web to leverage your local reputation may seem like a contradiction in terms, but that's exactly what many successful small businesses are doing today.

Curry Up Now, a San Francisco food-truck vendor specializing in Indian street food, is a perfect case in point. Owners Rana and Akash Kapoor started their business in 2009 with a single truck and a place marker on Google Maps. For the Kapoors, that place pin was more than just a nice added feature; it was a lifeline to their customers — especially after their reputation started to pick up steam in the local market.

The Kapoors then harnessed Twitter, Facebook, a website, blog, and mobile phone apps to make sure their customers found them every day and spread the word.

Wherever they went, the Kapoors made sure that the little pin on Google Maps followed them. They supplemented their location broadcasts with menu updates, event announcements, specials, photos, press coverage, and commentary.

Over the course of two years, Curry Up garnered more than 4,500 Facebook and 6,000+ Twitter followers, and expanded its operation to include additional trucks, as well as catering and online ordering.

Perhaps most importantly, Curry Up developed a custom interactive map that not only showed where its trucks were parked every day of the week but also allowed customers to search for their nearest location, and order online for pickup where it was convenient.

Today, Curry Up Now is arguably one of the most successful food truck operators in the San Francisco Bay Area, with four trucks and two recently opened brick-and-mortar restaurants.

Among the many lessons gained from this success story, making sure your business is found easily by the local market may be the most important. If people can place you geographically, they have an instant, tangible connection to you. In one simple step, you've connected your online and offline locations, providing customers with a cheat sheet of vital information: address and phone number, hours of operation, links to your website and social pages, contact numbers, and more.

If you're just starting to think about claiming your online real estate, many sites, including Google Maps, Yahoo, and Bing, offer free basic business listings with map locators.

Curry Up's success also underscores the need for small businesses in the digital age to think globally but act locally. According to Google research, 73 percent of consumers worldwide search for local businesses online.[11]

Everywhere you look, companies are trying to entice you with online deals for local shops, restaurants, theater tickets, and manicures. Real estate sites such as Zillow and Curbed allow you to (literally) look over your neighbor's fence. Hyperlocal news sites give you the lowdown on everything from high school band concerts to menu specials at neighborhood eateries.

Like Curry Up, once you've seen how big an impact a small map listing can have in your local market, it's likely you'll want to extend your reach further. Search ads, for instance, improve the odds that your location (as opposed to your competitor's) comes up in the sponsored results column when people look for products and services in your area.

That's exactly what Jay Lesiger, owner of the Chelsea Pines Inn in Greenwich Village, New York, discovered when he implemented an AdWords campaign. Plugging in key search terms such as guest house, Chelsea, New York and meatpacking district hotel, he was able to boost his hotel's online presence to the point where "guests now come in, smart phone in hand, saying, 'I just Googled you. Do you have any rooms available tonight?' "

AdWords also allowed him to see how many impressions (views) his ad received, how those impressions lead to contacts, and even how many people take action based on their views, so he can make the most effective use of his budget. "I like having the flexibility to budget what we need, when we can, as we need to," says Lesiger.

Putting in as little or as much time and money as your schedule and budget allows, and being in charge of the pace of your growth are additional benefits of search advertising. Once the ads start paying off, you can use that revenue to improve your placement, increase your frequency, or build your client base on a regional or national level.

We'll stop short of selling search advertising as some sort of miracle drug, but for many small businesses, it's indispensable. The best way to try it is just to jump in the pool and splash around. Many agencies are willing to help set up your campaign. Some work on commission; some charge an hourly rate; some will even negotiate a performance-based fee for new customers.

From local legend to global hero

Before the Internet age, the downsides for small businesses that wanted to reach across borders and acquire customers in other countries were obvious: language and cultural barriers, tariffs and trade issues, shipping and delivery costs, and of course, the danger of spreading yourself too thin.

Today, with the availability of online payment tools, streamlined processes, translation services, security measures, and easy overseas delivery options such as DHL and FedEx, serving an international clientele may be a far simpler task than you imagine. In fact, we believe that today's Internet tools enable small businesses to become multinational companies practically overnight.

Consider, too, the upsides of entering foreign markets. The Office of the United States Trade Representative reported that as of 2011, "roughly three-quarters of world purchasing power and almost 95 percent of world consumers [were] outside America's borders."[12]

Hiwave Dry Seafood is the online store of a dried seafood and traditional Chinese medicine business in Sai Kung, Hong Kong, run by three generations of the same family. In 2008, responding to the increasing popularity of online shopping in China and seeing a potential for growth, Hiwave opened an online store and was able to use its website to successfully expand into completely new customer segments in Hong Kong and beyond.

In the early days, its physical location served mostly older clientele who lived in its small fishing village. But with its website, Hiwave attracted a much broader range of customers interested in learning more about traditional medicines and herbs.

The online store also has brought global customers to the physical store, attracted in part by Hiwave's expertise and its descriptions of the history, preparation, and use of its products in Chinese customs and rituals. Stories and context not only helped build the company's credibility, it fostered customer loyalty and strengthened its reputation.

As a result, Hiwave now serves a much younger demographic across Hong Kong and around the world, with 60 percent of its online business coming from overseas — specifically the United States, Australia, and Europe — where these products are in high demand but not easily found.

Australians Mike Knapp and Michael and Jodie Fox's product was not tied to any specific region, so their website had to serve as an international ambassador from the get-go. The three founders envisioned their custom-design shoe company, Shoes of Prey, as a way to share the fun and creativity of the design process with shoe lovers around the world. The website they created allowed people to choose their own style, materials, colors, and decorations, using a handy online design tool.

The first customers were trusted friends, who tested the online tool and proudly wore their personalized designs. With their friends' seal of approval, the trio then enlisted the help of a popular YouTube fashion and makeup video blogger, who did an episode about their shoes. Almost overnight, they went "viral," becoming the talk of the Internet.

"We got half a million viewers [from that video]. That tripled our sales permanently," recalls Jodie Fox. Soon, the website began to get inquiries from overseas locations. The team quickly enabled it to receive foreign currencies so they could process international sales. Then, they launched a Google Search advertising campaign to promote Shoes of Prey to their fellow Australians.

As they expanded internationally, new campaigns targeted English-speaking countries, and they followed up with ads targeting those new locations: Canada, Ireland, New Zealand, and the United Kingdom.

"Despite being based in Australia," Knapp says, "It only took a matter of days for our first orders to start coming in from the other side of the world."

Currently, about 40 percent of the company's sales come from international buyers. One of the main reasons the owners say they've been successful with foreign audiences is their ability to edit ad text for each location. Knapp says they used Google's Insights for Search (now Google Trends) to identify each country's peak search traffic dates for various special occasions.

Trends also let them compare search volume patterns across specific categories, time frames, and products.

> Google Trends is a free tool that helps businesses track and compare popular search terms and keywords over time and across different locations. By analyzing which terms are used most often, businesses can tailor their marketing campaigns to run in the places and at the times of year when interest is highest.

"We time specific campaigns to target [events like] Mother's Day, which is on a different day in different countries," explains Knapp. "We run ads at different times of the year and edit the ads so they appeal to users in those countries."

After only a year of operation, the founders were able to hire three new employees. They've also added Japanese and Russian versions of their website, complete with local marketing and customer support, and they've formed partnerships with firms in those countries to help localize their offering.

The next step for Shoes of Prey, says Knapp, will be to use the Google Display Network, which lets them create ads from a variety of media (including text, image, and video) to inspire shoe lovers around the globe to design their own footwear.

New approaches for an infinite market

Let's put a bookmark there for a moment, and consider what this means for small businesses just venturing out online. Looking at the marketplace, we see a connected world. The web has expanded the customer base for small businesses to approximately two billion, all of whom can potentially be reached in a matter of months or a few years, as opposed to the decades it would have taken in the pre-digital age.

As the world becomes the marketplace and borders continue to disappear, creativity, originality, and the ability to evolve become paramount.

Emilio Concas is a shepherd in Sardinia, Italy, who used the reach of the Internet to usher his ancient profession into the 21st century. In 2005, Concas and his sons were grappling with an economic recession. To keep the business alive, they decided to create a website that asked people to adopt a sheep from their farm for less than 400 euros per year and become virtual shepherds from home.

Adoptive breeders got the rights to name their sheep, and also received sheep products such as Pecorino cheese and wool sweaters, along with periodic sheep status reports. Concas' online venture, Sardinia Farm (sardiniafarm.com) not only saved his farm from going under, it helped it grow and thrive in new ways.

Through search ad campaigns and social media, including an informational video about its operation on YouTube (which is fast approaching 10,000 viewers), Sardinia Farm's online activity has helped it snag customers from as far away as Rome, Florence, and even neighboring France.

Lastly, here's an example of how rethinking your business model for a global audience can breathe new life into an outmoded or faltering enterprise. Marie-Louise Holl got her start in 1984 manufacturing clogs, one of Holland's most well-loved and well-traveled national products. But beloved as they are, they are also about as common in Holland as Gouda cheese and narrow canals. Holl watched several close competitors go bankrupt because their businesses failed to adapt.

So, she decided to branch out and take Holl's Souvenir & Clogs from a simple footwear company to one that markets clogs as a concept and lifestyle — putting the clog stamp on everything from miniature key chains to chairs. These specialty clogs are now Holl's main draw as she acquires new retailers.

Her clog products can also be personalized, so they appeal to wholesalers, wedding parties, and big corporations. Using the power of the web, Holl's clogs have become fun accessories, fashion statements, corporate gifts, and souvenirs.

In 2009, on the store's 25th anniversary, Holl started dabbling with search advertising to see if she could reach an even broader overseas market. As it turned out, there was a large global demand for this fashion item, and the store was soon flooded with new product requests.

"I'm still amazed how eager our customers are from abroad, especially in Japan," she says. "Search advertising makes selling the concept extremely easy around the world." Her products are still stamped Made in Holland, but now they're sold all over the world.

We know this doesn't answer all the concerns you may have about international expansion. Translating your site into 12 different languages, for instance — even with the world's best translation service — is far from a perfect science, and you'll do well to have someone who speaks the native tongue preview content before posting it.

But many of the formidable hurdles that used to face businesses going global have now been pushed aside. Accepting secure payments in foreign currency, providing customer service, handling returns, and shipping are all today just a normal part of doing business online.

What's clear about these success stories is that the web is providing forward-thinking businesses with the tools they need to innovate, iterate, and challenge other business-as-usual companies in their sector. More people online means more potential customers — people who may very well be attracted to different, unusual, even eccentric ideas precisely because they are not just like everyone else's.

Many companies that started out locally — Tom's of Maine, Ben & Jerry's ice cream — have gone on to become the neighborhood shops of the world.

With the help of the Internet, yours could be next.

CHAPTER 4

The Social Explosion
Finding your voice in the worldwide conversation

Social media, in a nutshell, comes down to conversations. For the average consumer, that might mean everything from talking about a fantastic dinner he or she had at a restaurant to commenting on politics, spreading news of a major global event, or sharing a favorite music video, dry cleaner, or pizza-delivery service.

In our opinion, whether the conversation takes place on Twitter, Google+, Facebook, YouTube, Yelp, or some other social platform is less important than how that conversation is conducted, with whom, and what your customers do as a result of it.

For business owners, social media is often seen as the big chattering elephant in the room. You may not know exactly how to use it, but you can't ignore it. Why? Because social networks have viral power — the ability to get and spread information and opinion to millions of people in a matter of minutes. Remember the news about Osama Bin Laden's death? Twitter broke the story around the globe at 5,000 tweets per second — a full eight minutes before any of the mainstream media got wind of it.

In the world of commerce, there are more than 2.4 billion conversations about brands taking place every day in the United States. This new level of conversational reach has created overnight global sensations as well as tidal waves of negativity — clearly a double-edged sword for businesses of any size.

Here are some other social statistics to consider:

- 70 percent of Americans say they look at reviews before taking the next step to conversion.[13]

- Website visitors who interact with both reviews and customer questions and answers are twice as likely to purchase while visiting.

- The average consumer mentions specific brands over 90 times per week in conversations with friends, family, and coworkers.

- Consumer reviews are nearly 12 times more trusted than descriptions that come from manufacturers. [14]

Does this mean you should sink all of your time and marketing dollars into getting followers on Twitter or 'likes' on your Facebook page? We don't think so. Social marketing is nothing new. Historically, trade and commerce have always been social. Anybody who has been to an Indian or Turkish bazaar or a Sunday farmers' market can attest to that. What has changed, however, is scale and pace.

We believe social marketing is primarily about leveraging the effect of positive feedback to grow your customer base. Everything else is tools and tactics (and social marketing is therefore just one tool in your tool belt). Many small businesses — and companies in general — seem to be focused on driving large numbers of fans to their social pages. In our opinion, most small companies don't need a gazillion customers to be successful, just a manageable number of customers that matter.

Even Facebook admits that clicks don't necessarily convert to sales, especially for big-brand marketers. A recent study conducted by data-mining firm Datalogix for Facebook found that less than 1 percent of offline sales was tied to ad clicks.[15]

Being able to segment your customer base easily into clear "circles" is really key. Your best customers are not the same as people who have just clicked on 'like' or added themselves to a fan page. And you'll want to engage with those customers in a very different way than you would a casual browser.

There's an old axiom: It is better to excite a few than to leave a million cold. We strongly support this point of view when it comes to social marketing. Imagine walking into a room full of people you've never met and asking them to like you. Ridiculous, no? It's no different online.

So, what do customers want from their favorite brands online? How do they want to interact with them? Does a bad review or a negative comment spell doom for a small business? Or is there a way to harness that energy, engage that consumer, and convert him or her into a loyal customer? And how does a small business with limited resources find time to manage all its social media channels?

In the following sections, we'll try to answer some of these questions and target the primary ways small businesses can use social media to build brand loyalty, as well as point out the pitfalls.

State Bicycle Company: Facebook win

This small Arizona-based bicycle manufacturer had two clear goals when it came to Facebook: it wanted to drive brand engagement so customers would make the leap from Facebook to its website, and it wanted to increase its conversion rates.

State populated its Facebook page with product photos, company news, and regular events. It paid for sponsored stories in an effort to reach a broader audience and drive awareness. To engage its audience even further, the owners held photo caption contests, offered coupons, and released info on the newest products. Lastly, they explored the marketplace by testing keywords that included music preferences and names of direct competitors.

The results of their campaign: $500,000 in annual incremental sales from coupon codes and exclusive traffic, with 12 percent of website views coming by way of Facebook, and exponential growth in the number of people who 'liked' the shop's page — from 4,600 to 46,000+ within 12 months.[16]

Faulkner Packaging: Facebook fail

There are two sides to every coin. Peter Faulkner, owner of Faulkner Packaging, was advised to use social media to promote his company. But how many people will share with friends and family that they 'like' a certain brand of industrial paper product?

Faulkner set up a personal Facebook page and then secured the requisite 30 'likes' so he could set up a page for two of his main products. He expected the ball to keep rolling. Instead, it rolled to a stop. His initial success seemed attributable to a case of goodwill. So, he took the logical next step and pursued Facebook advertising.

Faulkner allotted a budget of roughly $50 a day for Facebook ads. Selecting the United Kingdom as a sole target and 24–60 as an age range, he turned up a respectable 178,000 people who would likely see the Faulkner Packaging ads. Almost immediately, the number of 'likes' went up on both pages.

But he was suspicious. Rather than invest more, Faulkner decided to pause the campaign on one page, and give the other the full budget. Can you guess what happened? The page without advertising stopped receiving any clicks. Even worse, for the $200 spent, the number of website visits originating from Facebook was exactly … two. That's $100 per click, and each of those visitors left after visiting his two pages.

[*Full disclosure: Faulkner is a longtime AdWords customer who's been setting up and testing campaigns since 2002. He recently looked at the source of all his hits on all his sites over the previous six months and found that Google, in its various domain formats, accounted for 92 percent of all visitors.*[17]]

Google+

With a multilayered approach to the idea of conversation, Google+, in our opinion, offers a more robust and effective way to manage your company's social presence. When you create a Google+ page, you create a place from which you can manage your company's web presence across multiple platforms, including Search, Maps and Mobile.

You also get a variety of tools to reach and target your customers, such as Circles, which lets you divide your customers and friends into different categories, and Hangouts, which let you interact with groups of friends and customers via live video chat.

North Bowl, a retro-themed bowling center in Philadelphia, found plenty to like using this social platform. Owner Oron Daskal, a guy who says he sees more high fives in a day than anyone else in Philly, was looking for a way to convey that fun, community feeling on the web.

He decided to launch a page for North Bowl on Google+ and began putting up posts that ranged from food-and-drink specials to information about live music and events. When the bowling alley held league tournaments, he and his staff streamed photos and videos, and posted updates to stir up excitement about league play. Daskal also separated his customers into Circles so he could tailor particular messages to specific groups of customers.

"I totally feel like we have a community here that is North Bowl, and if there's a way to move that from a physical place to a cyber-social space, that's a big step," says Daskal, who, with the help of his social pages, has gained fame around Philly for his Sunday Fundays and tasty Tater Tots. Daskal stresses that social media is a great tool for people to share their feelings about a place or service they love, and a great way for that business to hear valuable feedback and public opinion.

YouTube

Think fast: What's the world's second-largest search engine? If you said Yahoo or Bing, you're wrong. The answer is YouTube. At latest count, YouTube receives more than four billion views per day — more than 800 million of those on mobile devices — with 72 hours of video uploaded every minute. More video, in fact, is uploaded to YouTube in 60 days than the three major U.S. TV networks have created in 60 years.

This, in a nutshell, is your audience, equivalent to nearly half of the world's population. While the enormous size and reach of YouTube can feel overwhelming, it doesn't have to be. There are many ways to skin this giant cat.

In 2009 and 2010, Google looked at 32 different YouTube campaigns that ran in Germany. We found that YouTube added 3.4 percentage points of incremental reach compared to the reach of TV. But another number surprised us even more. We found a full 64 percent of viewers who saw an ad on YouTube had not seen the campaign on TV previously. They were all new viewers.

The overlap between viewers exposed to the same ad on TV and YouTube was only 1.9 percent. As a small business owner, this means that you can compete with much larger companies for a fraction of the cost. And you can imagine that these numbers will only become more significant as consumers spend more and more time online.

No one discounts the power of word of mouth to cement a company's reputation, but channels like YouTube take that basic construct and amplify it tenfold. A decade ago, if you found a great deal on something or an exceptional level of service, you might have told a friend or family member. Now, when the same thing happens, you can tell a thousand people at a time, and that thousand can tell a thousand more. That's what we mean by the power of viral.

Terrence Kelleman, founder of Dynomighty Design, realized early on how effective online video could be as a marketing tool. In 2001, he worked as a digital photographer for the Museum of Modern Art in New York, when he discovered magnets that shot together to form a straight line and realized he could make jewelry held together by magnetic force alone.

His first YouTube video of a magnetic bracelet was supposed to be a demo video for his website. Done in three or four takes, it was a simple point-and-shoot operation, using a Canon digital camera and a bracelet propped on a white background.

"In the original video, you can even hear the honking cars on Broadway outside our office," remembers Kelleman. He posted the minute-long video on YouTube that night and went home.

About a month later, he was sitting at his desk and heard the beep that alerts you to a new e-mail message. Then it beeped again and again — a total of 13 messages in less than a minute — notifying him of comments on his YouTube video.

"When I turned on my computer the next morning, it took an hour for all my e-mail messages to load," Kelleman says. "If you've ever imagined having a video go viral, this is how it starts."

Though rudimentary in quality, Kelleman's initial video did several things right. It focused on his product and clearly showed what the product could do. He kept the video to about a minute, a good length to match the average viewer's attention span. Lastly, he used an easy-to-operate digital camera with excellent HD video capabilities built in.

Dynomighty Design was inundated with orders, offers, and opportunities to expand its business. "Three months later, we'd finally caught up on all the orders, and our total sales in that time — following that one video — were approximately $130,000," says Kelleman. "Today, the video has almost three million views and continues to drive a steady flow of customers to our website."

Since posting that first video, Kelleman has uploaded 146 more and learned a lot about marketing. "To make an effective campaign, you need to have compelling visuals and content. We often look to other popular videos on YouTube for inspiration and ask ourselves, 'What do people like to watch?' When we see something we like, we implement aspects of that video into our own work, and try to build a connection with our customers that pictures and product copy can't really convey on their own."

Kelleman also uses YouTube Insight to learn about his viewers and gain their loyalty — including their demographics and how they find his videos. Today, many of his videos get more than 100,000 views within the first three months of being uploaded.

For small businesses, one of the most encouraging aspects of this story is that Kelleman didn't need to spend a fortune to make his video campaign successful. Because he shoots the videos himself, his primary investment has more to do with time than money. Using iMovie editing software on his MacBook Pro laptop (about $1,200), Kelleman now devotes anywhere from two hours to two days producing each video.

For more tips and tricks on how to create successful YouTube videos, download the YouTube Creator Playbook, http://www.youtube.com/yt/creators/playbook.html.

Twitter

While Facebook has its followers, Twitter — the social network in which people connect and comment on topics via 140-character text messages — has proved that less sometimes can be more.

San Francisco ice-cream company Humphry Slocombe found that combining the power of Twitter with review sites such as Yelp gave it a big edge in a crowded marketplace.

An unconventional ice-cream shop geared to grown-up tastes, Humphry Slocombe and its co-owners, Sean Vahey and Jake Godby, create more than a hundred flavors that rotate every day — sometimes even two or three times throughout the day. The shop began using free online marketing services, then invested further online because "there's no time gap between what [you want to] do and actually doing it," says Vahey.

Social media turned out to be a great research tool to announce products, flavors, and local happenings, as well as to bring in new customers and spread the ice-cream gospel to build a local fan base. Based on what people asked for on Yelp and Twitter, the duo added, eliminated, and even brought back flavors. Pretty soon their Twitter feed had more than 300,000 followers.

"I don't have a lot of time to do marketing or to sit down and actually reach out to people, but I'm able to get on the computer, and two minutes later, I've gotten the word out," says Godby. "We had no idea how much it would affect business. It just exploded."

Godby says online marketing also helped the shop reach an international audience and get press coverage in magazines such as *Gourmet*, *Food & Wine*, and *Bon Appétit*.

From conversation to conversion

Once you've started a dialog, the question then becomes, how do you promote your business and turn new fans into paying customers? The Nuyorican Poets Cafe used a combination of social tools to target and track its small-but-loyal existing base. In 2008, the café was a modest volunteer-led performance venue on New York's Lower East Side using paper flyers to publicize its events and not getting much traction. Executive Director Daniel Gallant decided to tap into social media to broaden the café's reach.

"Unlike some other arts venues, our demographic is very young, tech savvy, and diverse in every sense — geographically, economically, ethnically," Gallant says. "They don't necessarily have money to go buy a magazine or newspaper, but they will go online and see what their friends are doing."

In 2009, he launched a Nuyorican Facebook page and Twitter feed, and customized the Nuyorican Google+ Page (the business, brand, or organization listing, usually with a map, that is your public identity on Google+). He promoted his social presence at poetry slams and events by having event emcees remind audience members between acts to update their Twitter and Facebook status. Then, he reached out to opinion-influencer content sites such as Flavorpill, Thrillist, the Lo-Down, and Broadway World, using Google Alerts to track where the café got mentions.

His strategy boosted his online ticket sales by 30 percent and web traffic by 40 percent, and more than doubled the number of events the café hosts. Today, Nuyorican's Facebook page boasts nearly 18,000 members, and the café is a thriving cultural arts performing center with partnerships across the city.

Gallant says that many of the fears he had about social media marketing — that it would consume all of his time and that it would be difficult to keep track of — proved unfounded. "Small and medium-sized arts groups are intimidated by the number of sites, so they concentrate only on their own website," he says. "But the only cost in social media is effort, and it pays immediate dividends. When you consider that it can boost revenue and attendance, and make dialog with your constituents direct and straightforward, having a strong online presence actually saves time and effort."

Based on comments and feedback, Gallant gauges how particular artists or time slots have been received, and adjusts programming accordingly. "Being able to see the interests and needs of audiences in a real-time way can also dispel myths and conventional wisdom about what are or aren't good programming and operation procedures."

Ratings and reviews

The explosion of ratings and reviews online has changed not just how people get information, but how they shop, dine, travel, and do everyday tasks. Why would people make decisions based on the opinions of a single stranger, you ask? They don't. They make decisions based on the many opinions of people much like themselves. A 2011 Google study reported that 37 percent of U.S. shoppers find online social sources to be an influential driver when making decisions. The study also found that shoppers' top online social activities were:

1. Getting an online referral from a friend.
2. Becoming a friend or follower of a brand.
3. Reading blogs where the product was discussed.
4. Seeing the brand mentioned on a social networking site.

Brett Hurt, co-founder of Bazaarvoice, a clearinghouse for social communities and brand marketing, puts it this way:

"Word of mouth online has got to become part of the central nervous system for every company. Word of mouth is the medium we've been using since the tribal days to talk about essential knowledge. Where's the hunting good? Where's the fishing good? How do you not get eaten by the saber-toothed tiger?"

Today's tribal members are talking about your product every day on a dozen sites you've heard of and a thousand sites you haven't. There are star ratings, reviews, and raves online for every detergent, multivitamin, and Snuggie in your local drugstore.

Look up any university in the country, and you can find out who's the most popular history professor.

There is one critical difference between old-fashioned word of mouth and the digital version. "Talking over the hedge is one-to-one," says Professor Dave Reibstein of the Wharton School. "Digital word of mouth is one-to-millions. If you have a good experience, it's shared and re-shared with millions. You post it, and suddenly, it's flying."

If the idea of online ratings and reviews makes you queasy, you're in good company. Businesses small and large are cautious about opening up their sites and social pages to user comments. What if somebody says something negative? What if a whole lot of people do?

"We've found that the worldwide average for product reviews is a 4.3 out of 5.0," says Hurt. The math is simple enough: People like to talk most about the products they love the most. The flip side of the coin does exist, of course, especially in the restaurant industry. But even bad reviews don't have to be all bad. "People are scared to death of messaging not being all positive," says Reibstein. "But negative comments add authenticity."

The truth is, negative reviews increase conversion rates for all kinds of businesses because people see them and realize they're shopping in a truthful environment. If a company's reviews are all glowing, would you believe they're written by real people? And as they say in showbiz: There's really no such thing as bad publicity.

Social media: Last considerations

In addition to the many tangible benefits outlined above, there are a number of indirect advantages that small businesses can gain from marketing through social media, among them:

1. Deeper customer relationships

While many small businesses already have a relationship with customers from daily in-person interactions, social media expands these conversations into an online forum that offers owners more quantifiable knowledge of your customer base. By hosting a Hangout (live video chat) in Google+, for instance, you can offer customers a personal and interactive way to connect to your business, build loyalty, and share your expertise.

2. Broader base

Social media can extend your brand personality, offering your customers a tangible way to get involved. When people interact with you, they form a relationship. That relationship leads to loyalty, which then creates brand advocates, which quickly broadens your customer base.

3. New ways to reward loyalty

Social media is an excellent way to say thank-you. If last weekend's event was a total success, you can say so, and you can thank people for their support. Even customers who may have missed the sale will appreciate the gesture, and when they hear about all the great deals they missed, they may very well come in the following week.

4. Insights and feedback

"Crowdsourcing" — using your customers as a focus group to research and test new ideas and products — is a great way to get valuable feedback and generate excitement quickly about upcoming products. If you want to increase the number of responses, consider offering an incentive such as a discount or prize. Either way, customers enjoy knowing their opinion matters.

5. More engaged customers

Social media can keep you engaged in the community. Two good ways to get involved are by supporting local events and joining local business organizations. By becoming friends with other businesses online, your company will strengthen the fabric that holds such offline communities together. Once you participate, post about it. Give consumers a reason to pay attention to you.

6. A platform for showing off expertise

You're already a subject-matter expert. Thought leadership is powerful, and more customers will support your company if they feel that you care about your craft. So, become a resource, and broadcast your knowledge. When something interests you within your field, post about it.

7. A way to share positive reviews

Arguably, the best thing about social media is the flood of positivity coming from happy customers. Especially in urban centers, businesses have been known to get huge boosts based on reviews. Happy customers also can post useful content (photos, videos) that has unmistakable authenticity, and they do it free of charge.

8. A face for your business

Nobody wants to support a nameless, faceless corporation. People want to relate to real people. The number one way to send this message is by responding to comments and mentions from your customers promptly. By taking an active role in social media, you'll send the message that you're listening and that you care.

What's Different About You?
How small brands stand out in a crowd

The digital age has ushered in a world of unbroken connectivity, nonstop entertainment, and innumerable ways to save 30 seconds. It has also made our lives more complicated, presenting us with a plethora of options we never knew existed and a thousand products we never knew we needed.

According to Yankelovich Consumer Research, we've gone from being exposed to about 500 marketing messages a day in the 1970s to as many as 5,000 messages per day today. What that means is that unless your customers have suddenly and dramatically increased their attention spans, many of those messages likely get lost in the shuffle.

As a small business owner, you want your product or brand to stand out from the crowd, but we don't think you can achieve that by shouting over the racket. Companies that treat social channels like a freeway do not add value, begin a dialog, or craft actual content, they merely create additional noise. And your customers will respond accordingly — most likely by tuning out.

With so much clutter, solid marketing principles become even more important. Don't speak just to be heard. Speak when you have something to say — a product launch, a sale, a new service, a new feature. The more you value your customers' time, the more they'll pay attention.

The first step is to figure out what you want to say. What is your biggest differentiator? The second step is to decide where and how to say it. The third step is to tie this information back into your business as a whole.

Rule #1:
Identify a real-world problem, then solve it

As a small business owner, your brand will be relevant to the degree your product adds value. In other words, you can build a brand around a product or service, but it doesn't work the other way. A brand makes a promise. Fulfilling that promise each and every day is the best approach to branding for small businesses. If you focus on your brand first, you're putting style before substance.

Kevin Plank, the former University of Maryland football player who founded Under Armour in 1996, built his multinational brand around a simple plan to make a better T-shirt.

As an athlete, Plank saw the need for more muscle support. So, he came up with the idea to build compression directly into the material. Plank also saw that athletes had no way to move sweat away from the skin, so he made fabric that wicked away moisture. Filling these two unmet needs became the basis for his company. As Under Armour has grown and the product lines have expanded, Plank has never strayed from his core mission — the needs of athletes. As a consequence of solving this real-world problem, the brand's reputation has become synonymous with performance gear for serious athletes around the world.

So, what's your mission? What problem do you help your customers solve? And how do you integrate this solution into a marketing message that drives your reputation and your brand? Whether you have a new business or an established one, making sure you focus on your product — and what sets it apart from your competitors' — should drive your marketing campaign.

Rule #2:
Be true to yourself

This may seem obvious, but if you're a plumber, you shouldn't be talking about restaurants. Businesses that honor the products and services they know and love, and keep their original mission at the core of everything they do — no matter how far it takes them — are much more likely to come across as authentic in the eyes of their customers.

A shining example of this comes from the outdoor gear and clothing company Patagonia. Founder Yvon Chouinard got his start in the 1950s hand-forging tools for his fellow mountain climbers. Over the decades, he and partner Tom Frost refined their climbing gear to make it "stronger, lighter, simpler, and more functional," as well as environmentally ethical.

By the 1970s, Chouinard Equipment had become the largest supplier of climbing hardware in the United States, and it started branching out into clothing. Pretty soon, clothing sales surpassed equipment production. The partners changed the name to Patagonia to reflect the shift but kept true to their mission to "build the best product, cause no unnecessary harm, and use business to inspire and implement solutions to the environmental crisis."

With pioneering materials such as polypropylene and eco-friendly Synchilla fleece, Patagonia's clothing lines soon became the standard-bearer not just for technical outdoor clothing but for environmental stewardship.

As the years went by, no matter what detours the business took or how it branched out, the company stayed true to its core values, believing that credibility with its customers was paramount to its success. The partners' instincts were right. At the height of the economic recession in 2009–2010, Patagonia posted its two most profitable years ever.

"We've made many mistakes, but we've never lost our way for very long," the company explains in its Patagonia Company history. "Although we first intended Patagonia as a way to free ourselves from the limitations of the original climbing business, precisely those limitations have kept us on our toes and helped us thrive."[18]

Rule #3:
Let your customers be part of the process

In today's hands-on, user-generated, reviews-driven culture, customers want meaningful relationships with the brands they care about.

My Starbucks Idea is an online community within Starbucks Coffee in which customers can offer product and business ideas, vote, and comment on how they feel things are going.

Community moderators, called Idea Partners, curate the most innovative ideas and then present them to key decision makers within the company.

As of June 2011, more than 110,000 ideas had been submitted, of which 150 have been implemented. Making sure its customers know they're valued and giving them a role in the company's success are key ways Starbucks has stayed atop the very crowded gourmet coffee market.

Another good example comes from Peeps — those adorable puffy marshmallow Easter candies. Not only did the parent company, Just Born, include its fans in its marketing strategy, it let customers lead the charge. In the process, Peeps went from an old-fashioned Easter treat to an icon of popular culture.

When fans started using Peeps to create dioramas and animated videos, the company not only embraced the idea, it began sponsoring diorama contests of its own — even providing prize packages.

Likewise, after years of having customers ask for a brick-and-mortar store, Just Born granted their wish and opened retail outlets in Washington, D.C., Minnesota, and Pennsylvania. As a result, Peeps have turned a niche business into a global conglomerate that produces more than a billion treats a year.

Rule #4:
Channel your passion

Assuming that your product or service grew out of passion, your business will become a natural extension of that. How you convey that passion is the way that you can differentiate yourself from the competition.

Take the age-old rivalry between soft drink companies Coke and Pepsi. Each makes a nearly identical product, yet each has its own loyal following. Why is that? The answer has less to do with flavor than you might think (*see more about this in Chapter 8*).

People are drawn to Coke or Pepsi based on subtle distinctions in how the companies position each product and how they channel that to their customers.

Coke has built its brand around selling happiness. It has been steadfast, consistent, and timeless in its messaging. "Have a Coke and a Smile," "Things Go Better With Coke," and "I'd Like to Teach the World to Sing," are all ad campaigns targeting the joy that people feel when they drink Coke.

Pepsi's message, on the other hand, has revolved around innovation, reinvention, and a willingness to change with the times. Pepsi has redesigned its logo innumerable times and championed slogans such as, "The Choice of a New Generation," "Be Young, Have Fun, Drink Pepsi," and "Live for Now."

Both brands have their merits, but how they envision themselves and express that vision to the public is what makes each brand unique.

On a smaller scale, Florida-based YOLO, a stand-up paddleboard (SUP) company founded in 2005, channeled its passion for a new sport into a lifestyle that it marketed to followers. YOLO owners Jeff Archer and Tom Losee were avid paddleboarders who wanted to share their love of the sport and make it accessible to others — regardless of age or skill level.

Rather than using other people's boards, Archer and Losee decided to make their own, crafting a wider, longer, and more stable SUP that could be used by anyone. YOLO, which stands for You Only Live Once, now sells 18 different kinds of boards to accommodate water conditions and paddler types, and has become identified with the sport — its brand practically interchangeable with the term paddleboarding.

The owners channeled their passion (and hence their brand) even further by sponsoring and leading demo events, lessons, and races, and by making boards available for rent at resort communities. There's even an iPhone app to help connect people to stand-up paddleboard events around the country.

Tying the company name and motto into its marketing, lifestyle, and the paddleboard community at large, YOLO has come to embody the sport in a way that is unique and ultimately profitable.

The practicalities of building a brand

So far, we've talked in broad terms about what branding means to a small business. But what does it look like on a practical level? For any small company trying to establish its identity, three elements must come into play: crafting your story, creating a mythology, and letting your expertise shine through.

What do you know about and care about that you could easily share? Why did you pick this particular path? What is it about your process, your service, your product that you consider best in class? Answering these questions will help you get a feel for your circle of greatest influence, which is a critical part of breaking through the clutter and developing a loyal following.

David Garland, host of the Internet-based "The Rise to the Top: The #1 Non-Boring Business Show," believes that to be truly successful as a small business owner, you can't merely have customers, you need fans: people who know you, like you, trust you, and most importantly, are willing to spread the word about you.

To build this community, small business owners must create useful content, keep readers interested, and provide a good enough reason to keep them coming back. Here are a few additional pointers from Garland about creating successful content:

1. Creating a blog (a series of online articles, entries, photos, or web links that showcases your knowledge or offers additional information related to your business) is a good way to engage viewers. A few short paragraphs with practical tips, insights, or trends should do the trick. This should be bite-size content, consumable in a single sitting. Photos, designs, even a concept sketched on a napkin are also appropriate for this channel. Ask yourself: Is it useful? Is it inspiring? Is it fun? If yes, post it, and get on with your day.

2. One of the biggest mistakes businesses make is spending too much time creating content and not enough time ensuring customers actually see it. The numbers don't have to be huge. Even 20 people might be enough, as long as they're the right 20.

3. OK, it happens. A company goes to great lengths to post quality content, customers see it, and then ... crickets. It's not a reason to panic. But fixing this requires some honest introspection on the part of the business owner. Could your content be too self-promotional? Is it boring? Is the time span between posts inconsistent? Are you responding to the comments your customers leave? Interaction breeds loyalty. And while it may take awhile to find the right mix of content, it's probably not as time-consuming as you might think. And the payoff is priceless.

Bruno Bornsztein, founder of Curbly, an online community for do-it-yourself home designers, is a great example of how to make online marketing and subject expertise work hand in hand. Bornsztein launched Curbly because, "After years of fixing, mending, patching, and decorating my first home, I wanted to create a place online where people could celebrate all the hard work they put into their homes."

Using a combination of how-to articles, photos and videos, inspiring success stories, blogs, tips, and member forums, Bornsztein developed a space where DIYers could share their stories, go for advice and assistance, and get ideas and inspiration.

Since the beginning, he has used display advertising to generate enough revenue to keep the community humming. Today, the website receives almost 500,000 visitors a month, with display ads generating $3,000 to $5,000 a month — enough to allow him to contract eight or nine freelance writers and topic experts on a regular basis.

Curbly has also launched a spin-off series of how-to manuals that offer in-depth, graphic tutorials on completing DIY projects at home. "The coolest thing about it," Bornsztein says, "is that the products I use on the page match the ads really tightly, so it provides an incentive for me to create high-quality content."

We can learn several things from Bornsztein's success. One, quality content will keep people coming back. Two, expertise is valuable — something both consumers and advertisers are willing to pay for. And three, you don't necessarily need to create the content yourself. Re-posting, re-tweeting, and sharing links from reliable, trusted sources can be equally effective.

One more example comes from the food blog Smitten Kitchen. The online passion of journalist Deb Perelman, Smitten Kitchen grew out of her love for great food, but it wasn't until Perelman began writing about and photographing her recipes that the blog really took off. Perelman's natural, accessible communication style made everything she did in the kitchen seem fun.

Accolades began pouring in from the likes of Gwyneth Paltrow, Martha Stewart, and a small army of other influential bloggers. By 2008, Perelman was able to quit her day job, and she hasn't looked back since. Her advice for aspiring bloggers:[19]

1. **Make sure you love what you're talking about** and convey that passion to your audience.

2. **Have fun exploring your world.** If you love the subject, it shouldn't be a chore. Follow a thread, see where it leads, and take people there with you.

3. **Only share the absolute best information.** If readers get the feeling your content is generic or dated, it can do more harm than good.

4. **Say what you mean, and be prepared to stand behind it.** Comments and feedback are great ways to learn more about your readers, but to really drive the dialog, you'll need to have your own opinion.

5. **Do it because you want to.** Will it help you drive profits? Probably. But that can't be the primary driver for the blog.

CHAPTER 6

Some Things Never Change
Why timeless principles still apply

R oy Amara, Stanford researcher and former president of the Institute for the Future, famously said, "We tend to overestimate the effect of a technology in the short run and underestimate the effect in the long run." This truism, referred to as Amara's Law, offers a number of lessons for today's small businesses.

Predicting the future is not an easy task, but hindsight is 20-20. Looking back, it's easy to play Monday morning quarterback about products and ideas that seemed promising but never took off. Remember Macintosh TV? Qwikster? Motorola Xoom? Early adopters — those people who jumped on the latest-product bandwagon before it had established a successful track record — were essentially experimenting. And not every experiment pays off.

From a marketing perspective, we've had hundreds of years of magazine, radio, billboard, and television campaigns to reflect on, learn from, and improve upon since the first newspaper ad appeared in 1673. So, you would think we'd have established a set of tried-and-true best practices.

And yet, we are constantly amazed at how often modern campaigns follow the worst practices, jumping on the trend of the moment, blowing their marketing budgets on unproven products and methods.

The truth is, even in the digital age, most basic marketing principles still apply. The number of products aimed at small business owners has expanded, but your customers are still human beings, which means the factors influencing their purchasing decisions haven't changed that much.

Drawing from our own experiences working across various industries, in places ranging from the United States and Russia, to Africa and Norway, we'd like to offer a set of timeless tenets to serve as guideposts — principles that despite all our technological advances continue to apply across all markets and segments.

Principle One:
Action beats attitude

When it comes to your customers, the bottom line is: Behavior matters; attitudes don't. Despite the current prevailing sentiment or social flavor of the day, and despite what people say they like or don't like, it's what they actually *do* that counts.

If you went back 20 years and asked people whether or not they needed mobile phones, they would have questioned your sanity. If you went back 10 years and asked if they needed another social network, the response would have been about the same.

When the mobile cassette player Sony Walkman first came out, the marketplace shrugged. Early editions didn't test well, and Sony predicted it would only sell about 5,000 units a month. In the first two months, people snapped up more than 50,000 units, and Sony went on to sell 200 million over the next 30 years.[20]

We're not saying your customers are dishonest — just that they don't always know what they want. And in a research setting, they tend to project the kind of person they want to be: rational, considerate, armed with an uncanny ability to make logical decisions.

In reality, most people are prone to making emotional, even irrational decisions when it comes to purchasing. So, rather than relying on what they say, you should be looking at what they actually do as a way to guide your marketing strategy.

Principle Two:
Product comes before brand

Deliver a superior product for a good price, and it will drive your brand recognition. The best marketing campaigns don't just capitalize on people's desires to be current, hip, or relevant, they offer a fundamental truth. Put something on the market that's good, and you significantly decrease the amount of time and money necessary to market it.

With the proliferation of reviews and comparison sites, brand loyalty is fast becoming a thing of the past. Consumers today are driven increasingly by the tangible things a product delivers — performance, value, latest and greatest features — and are less influenced by catchy names, clever jingles, and cute logos.

Warby Parker, a company that offers simple, understated, quality eyeglasses for under $100, is a great example of this principle. It was founded on the idea that prescription eyewear shouldn't be so expensive and "everyone has the right to see." Warby Parker designs its own frames and cuts out the middleman by selling directly to customers through its website.

The company also commits to donating a pair of glasses to someone in need for every pair of glasses it sells. The combination of good quality, good price, and good deeds has been a marketing knockout punch. Without spending a dime on advertising, the company beat its yearly sales projections in 21 days. It has grown 500 percent since launching in 2010, with a reported 50 percent of the company's sales driven by word of mouth.[21]

Another company that began with humble, even misguided beginnings is Flickr, one of the Internet's most popular online photo-management and -sharing applications.

The company got its start in 2004 as a massive web-based role-playing game. Within the game was a chat room, Flickr Live, that featured a tool that let players share photos and post them to a web page. Users were lukewarm about the game, but they loved the photo-sharing aspect.

So founders Stewart Butterfield and Caterina Fake dumped the game and focused on the photo application. Within a few years, Flickr's photo streams included the official White House photographer and the Library of Congress, and by 2011, Flickr had a total of 51 million registered members and 80 million visitors.[22]

Moving from a game company to a photo-sharing phenom required an entirely new mindset. The brand, in this case, was irrelevant until Flickr established itself in the photo-sharing space.

Principle Three:
What gets measured gets done

In 2008, Olympic swimmer Michael Phelps beat out his competition in the 100-meter butterfly by 0.01 seconds. Imagine, if you will, that same race without a timekeeping device. Not only would we never know who won, Phelps might not have given that final push. In other words, what can't be proven isn't worth fighting for.

The same metaphor applies to your business, with metrics serving as the device that determines how well your business is performing. When you begin to measure the right metrics and key performance indicators, you introduce objectives, and more importantly, a culture to improve on those objectives.

The mistake we think many small businesses make is to pay more attention to cash flow and short-term profitability than to long-term factors. We recommend you worry less about micromanaging the books and more about a few key indicators, such as where your customers come from, what products and content are most important to them, and which areas show the most potential for increasing revenue and customer retention while reducing costs.

Take the example of the San Francisco Museum of Modern Art (SF MoMa) — among the first in its industry to get online. After several years, however, the museum still had significant digital blind spots. Many key investments such as audio, video, and specialized web content performed well, but the museum had no clear way to track usage, so it had trouble determining which of these methods was most successful. SF MoMa also was unable to measure revenue or product sales from the online store.

The museum hired an adviser who used Google Analytics to find out which content visitors liked best on the website and which parts of the store were performing best. By looking at the most popular areas, the museum gained a 15 percent increase in traffic accuracy, which allowed it to make more confident data-driven decisions. SF MoMa then tied its marketing campaigns to actual sales conversions, which increased its profitability.

Principle Four:
Choose your channels carefully

We have two recommendations here. The first: Start with what's free. Only after those bases are covered should you consider paid options. The second: Only go into less-efficient channels once you've maxed out the most efficient ones.

Winning on the web is not about guesswork. Today, businesses have a variety of ways to determine their best channel choices. Track potential channels through an analytics program to see which generate the most clicks. Talk to your customers and find out how they prefer getting their information — through e-mail, from your website, via video? See what your competition uses successfully, and assess whether that could work for you.

Armed with new information, you'll quickly realize that a structured, programmatic approach can work wonders. We do, of course, recognize that measuring takes time and requires attention, and that there might be easier methods (relying on gut instinct, for example), but we believe ultimately you'll be rewarded for your efforts.

Principle Five:
Conversion, conversion, conversion

Statistics show that average online conversion rates vary between 1 percent and 12 percent. Even for a company at the low end, a small improvement — say to 1.2 percent — equates to a full 20 percent increase in sales. The opposite is also true: If prospective buyers come into your store but don't convert into paying customers, you may not be in business for long.

Take a step back, then, and think about what happens when a potential customer enters your store. What makes him happy? What makes her spend more? Choose a goal, and find a way to measure it.

Most businesses focus on driving prospects to their online or offline stores, and seem less concerned with what happens once these potential customers get there. But all efforts are useless if you don't turn a lead into a sale, and turn that customer into an advocate for your brand.

The steps along the way to achieving these goals are called micro-conversions. Amazon approaches its customer acquisition this way. Not everyone will buy something every time, but you still need to engage those people, and keep them as loyal customers. Sending them gift suggestions, newsletters, letting them know when new inventory arrives or when items are discounted — are all ways of motivating customers to purchase down the road.

Principle Six:
Your best customers are the ones you already have

You've likely heard this one before, but it's a principle that never goes out of fashion. According to a report in the *Harvard Business Review*, "Companies can increase profits by almost 100 percent if 5 percent more of their customers are retained." The report also claims, "It's six to 10 times cheaper to keep a current customer than to add a new one." Take it from a couple of marketing guys: The best campaign is the one you never have to run.

Chris Zane, owner of Zane's Cycles and author of *Reinventing the Wheel: The Science of Creating Lifetime Customers*, went so far as to put a monetary value on his customers. He calculated that each of them was worth $12,500 to his company over his or her lifetime. Once he had this valuation, he was able to make more rational, logical decisions about which aspects of his business added or subtracted from this value. Zane has had an average growth rate of 23.5 percent over the past 30 years.

What he realized early on was that he was not just selling bike frames, tires, and spokes, but an experience. His bike business might go up and down, but his customers were enduring. "If I don't make money on one particular transaction, but the customer is happy, they'll come back over and over and over again," he said in an interview with *Inc.* magazine. "We're looking at the lifetime value of the customer."[23]

Zane also implemented a host of customer-pleasing policies and services, such as 90-day price protection and lifetime service guarantees. And he installed a coffee bar in his shop so he could offer his customers free drinks.

So, how are you measuring customer satisfaction? The minute you start paying attention is the moment things will begin to change. Ask customers a few simple questions. Give them a small discount in return for their time, or choose another way to say thank-you. When you learn what they need, act on it. A variety of customer satisfaction tools, many of which used to be expensive, are now available at little or no cost. A customer who knows his or her voice is heard is a happy customer.

CHAPTER 7

Performance Tracking 2.0
How data is changing the game

Most business owners hear the words *performance tracking* and begin to yawn, conjuring visions of graphs and charts, and number-crunching technogeeks dancing their way across a digital stage. Understandably, measurement and analysis aren't as tangible or sexy as increasing website traffic, showing up first in search engines, or getting more people to like you on Facebook.

But as mundane as it may sound, if you're not using the power of the web to track your performance, you're not letting the Internet do what it does best. Can you imagine Wall Street without the omnipresent ticker board? The same holds true for your website if you don't know who's visiting or what they're doing when they get there. In the words of renowned management consultant Peter Drucker: You can't manage what you don't measure.

Twenty years ago, market research and analysis were something you could *only* do as a big company with deep resources. Even 10 years ago, much of the data you can access easily today would have been prohibitively expensive for a small company.

Today, businesses have a whole new world of real-time customer data available to them — data that with a modest amount of effort and minimal cost (or no cost at all) can give an instant picture of the quantity and quality of visitor traffic and trends, and how it stacks up against the competition.

Armed with this information, it's easy to assess what's working and what's not, and make adjustments that will improve your customers' experience, and ultimately your online performance. Not only do you no longer require a research department, you don't even need an office.

As we enter the teen years of the 21st century, more and more companies also are talking about *big data* and its impact on the bottom line. In broad terms, big data refers to analyzing enormous volumes of transactions, clickstreams, social media activity, phone data, and other statistics to find patterns that can help predict market trends accurately and improve performance.

A recent article on big data by Andrew McAfee and Erik Brynjolfsson in the *Harvard Business Review* put it in plain terms: *Data-driven decisions are better decisions. …Using big data enables managers to decide on the basis of evidence rather than intuition.*

We couldn't agree more. Unlike the research studies of the past decade, which could be skewed depending on your viewpoint, hard data is completely objective. Focus on driving and improving your business's key performance indicators, and the rest will follow.

Google Analytics

We know it may sound self-serving to tout Google Analytics as the best free service we know for tracking and gathering data about your online audience, but it's a product we feel very passionate about — and so do many others in our industry.

In a 2010 report in *Inc.* magazine, 10 out of 10 web analytics experts rated it their favorite product on the market.

What does it do? Google Analytics generates statistics about visitors to your website, such as how they found you, where they came from, what they're doing while on your site, how often they return, and if they took an action that you consider valuable.

Here's a short primer of the many ways you can use Analytics to improve your online performance:

1. See where visitors come from

Knowing how your customers find you can be invaluable information when it comes to deciding which online products to use to promote your business. Analytics tools let you see how visitors arrived at your site, whether via a link on someone else's site, a search engine, Facebook, or a blog.

2. See which keywords customers use

Keywords are the words and phrases people use to search for a product and find a site. Say someone types in tennis shoes and ends up on your site, which specializes in cross-trainers. This report shows you the exact terms that visitor used when searching so that you can tailor and optimize your content to match those words. This is called search engine optimization (SEO).

3. See where customers spend the most time

Google Analytics can show you which content on your site is most attractive to visitors by tracking the most commonly viewed pages and how they're used. Once you have this information, you can delve much deeper, filtering the results by specific title words or analyzing such things as average time spent on a page.

4. Target your demographics

Several tools, including Google Trends, have proved extremely helpful in identifying and breaking down the types of people who visit your site by gender, age, ethnic background, and even geographic location. Once you know this information, you can target your efforts to appeal to these demographics directly.

5. Get more customers to convert

People often consider conversion a science, but if that's the case, it's an elementary one. Successful conversion just means that you need to test every element on your website religiously — including headlines, calls to action, social media connections, images, and videos — to see how effective each is. For instance, you may find that a headline that reads, "Welcome to Acme Furniture" leads to more conversions than one that simply says, "Acme Furniture."

How businesses use Analytics

The BBQ Guys began in Louisiana as a traditional brick-and-mortar shop and made the jump to online in 2001. But the owners felt they were losing a personal connection to their customers, so they turned to online video to bring back the human touch. They hired a local chef to be their on-air personality, and pretty soon, their combination of expert grilling advice, cooking products, and sizzling meat became a YouTube hit.

Along the way, they began using Google Analytics to track their campaigns, and insight tools from YouTube to figure out how to optimize their content and raise viewership.

By looking at the data, they realized that they lost viewers when their videos ran too long. By shortening their videos to three minutes and honing in on hot spots that viewers tended to watch again and again (such as images of food sizzling on the grill), they were able to slow their drop-off rate, and build their view count.

They also implemented YouTube's TrueView in-search and in-display tools, which utilize keywords, to put their videos in front of likely viewers who searched for barbecue information. Today, BBQ Guys is one of the web's leading online outdoor-cooking sites, growing from 800 to 900 views a day, to some 5,300, with a total of about 4.5 million views to date.

Terra Organics, a small, organic community-supported farm in Washington State that runs a produce home-delivery service, wanted to get more people signed up for its service, increase the effectiveness of its AdWords campaign, and maximize its ROI.

"While we had seen some great gains [using AdWords], we knew we weren't using it to its full potential and weren't sure how best to budget our ads for the most efficiency," explains Terra Organics owner Dan Hulse.

Using Analytics, Hulse and partner Elliot Trotter learned how to maximize their cost per click and not waste impressions so they could stretch their small budget. They also used negative keywords to differentiate their shop from competitors. Negative keywords work by making sure your business doesn't turn up in a search for something unrelated, in this case, a phrase like organic chemistry.

The company also linked its ads to its Google+ page so customers could immediately find the address. In one month, Terra got more than 100,000 impressions.

"By using Analytics, we experienced more desired results on our ads and a more even performance," says Hulse.

One last example comes from Louis Rossetto, CEO of TCHO, a small artisanal chocolatier in San Francisco. Rossetto used Analytics to make sure the right content reached the right audience.

"Web analytics enables you to understand where your customers are coming from, what they are doing on your site, and ultimately, what they care about," he says. "If you want to have a good connection to your customers, you have to understand who they are and what they do."

Cash Shurley, TCHO's director of IT, explains that the company optimized its website by targeting content based on what people viewed and what they bought. Analytics also helped TCHO see how long customers stayed on the site and where exactly they clicked.

"The ROI of Analytics is really high," Shurley says. "It's a free tool, and the only cost to us is the time it takes to analyze and utilize the data, so I'd say [the ROI] is upwards of 1,000 percent."

What to track and why

In our current roles at Google, we spend a lot of time helping business owners adopt digital technology, but time and again, we see that performance tracking is an afterthought, especially among small businesses.

Small companies caught up in the daily rigors of running a business, often focus too much on a single aspect, while their competition capitalizes on neglected sectors. The right data and measurements can ensure that you're seeing the big picture. Here are five key principles of performance tracking to keep in mind:

1. Track every step, not just the aggregate

At a financial services firm, we asked consumers to sign up online for a credit card. We saw that customers got to the sign-up page, but somewhere before completing the form, they dropped off. By doing an analysis, we discovered a single field, Time at Address, was the culprit.

Instead of telling us how long they had lived at their current address, some people entered the actual time of the day (which is of course slightly amusing but not terribly helpful). By adding a simple drop-down check box with the options 0–6 months, 6 months to 2 years, and 2 years and longer, we got the information we needed, and made it much simpler for consumers to sign up, thus improving our conversion rate.

It's a small but important lesson: Measurement is an effective way to identify success and failure at a granular level. Be sure to track every step.

2. Identify key metrics, and see how they're performing

To choose a key metric, ask yourself what problem you're trying to solve. It could be the number of new customers during a certain stretch of time. Or the number of a certain item sold. Or your cost-per-acquisition (CPA). Choose one, and start there.

Once you've identified your key metric, conducting an A/B test is a good way to see what's truly performing. Have you ever visited a restaurant website and been swept up in an elaborate photo montage set to a Bach concerto? While some restaurants may consider this a pleasing way to set the mood, it's just as likely a long musical introduction might put people off. The only way you'll know for sure is by doing a quick A/B test — one with and one without the music — and see which site gets and retains more visitor traffic.

Anytime you ask for information, you can bet performance tracking will help you streamline the experience. It comes down to being a good listener. Choose the right things to measure, and you'll have taken the first step to giving your customers a better overall experience.

3. Specify your benchmarks and choose your goal

What are you willing to spend for a new customer? Do you have a funnel, with customers at every stage? If the top of the funnel (new customers) is dry, maybe it's time to network. If the bottom is dry (customers are looking but not buying), it's a problem of conversion.

Say you've identified your cost-per-acquisition as $50. Is that the cost of getting a new customer? Or is that money going toward an existing customer and therefore being wasted? Identify what you're willing to spend on new and returning customers, and stick to that goal. Use analytics to see if you're meeting those benchmarks. Adjust, then try again.

4. Get context
Think about what you are measuring. If you launch a website and start to show an increase in calls, figure out what those calls are really about. For instance, if you're running a photography business, and your calls are about camera repair, the calls aren't helping your business. Without metrics and specific benchmarks to compare to, you'll likely mistake unqualified leads as a sign that your business is improving.

Conversions need context. More clicks are good, but you need to look beyond the click. That's another way A/B tests can come in handy.

5. Test and iterate
Iteration in this context refers to the continuous process of fine-tuning. Start with a hypothesis, test it, then adjust as necessary. Here's a simple example: Cashstore is a shopping engine that allows members to earn money on each purchase they make through the site. It's like a rewards card without the monthly bill.

Though 90 percent of Cashstore's visitors browse through the site's home page, Google Analytics revealed that the home page click-through rate to the registration form was low — only 2 percent to the sign-up page, 23 percent to the form. The team realized that the home page had usability problems.

Cashstore's search partner approached the problem by designing an A/B test of the home page, which it ran through

Google Website Optimizer. In the original home page, the Flash animation took a full minute to display a call to action before the sign-up form appeared.

A new design focused on presenting the same information clearly, with a more visible call to action. Version one recorded an extremely low conversion rate — just 3 percent. Version two produced the highest conversion rate on the sign-up form — a full 20 percent — which more than compensated for the lack of flashy animation. The better performing design went live and quickly generated a 25 percent increase in new sign-ups for Cashstore from the home page.

Ultimately, we see performance tracking as your insurance policy. Whether your marketing budget is big or small, the end result should be a good return on your investment. By analyzing the data, staying away from hunches and opinions, and adjusting your strategy based on solid metrics, you'll find you can improve your online performance dramatically — and save time and money in the process.

CHAPTER 8

Understanding Your Customers and Channels

Insights into the mind of the marketplace

In this chapter, we'll attempt to unravel an age-old mystery: Why do customers respond the way they do? Why do they pick Coke over Pepsi, puppies over kittens, the black Nike over the white one?

A number of factors go into the decision-making process, not all of them logical. According to Dan Ariely, Professor of Behavioral Economics and author of *Predictably Irrational: The Hidden Forces That Shape Our Decisions*, social pressure, expectations, emotions, too many choices, the power of suggestion, perceived cost, and lack of self-awareness all factor into making decisions that are less than rational.

In looking at the Coke vs. Pepsi question, for instance, Ariely notes that people's preferences have less to do with taste and more to do with visual and emotional connections. In a blind taste test conducted by neuroscientists, people chose Coke not because it was their favorite flavor, but because they associated the taste with the name, the color on the can, the brand, or even a memorable ad slogan.

Another factor to consider: Your customers don't necessarily know what they want (until you give it to them). As automobile maker Henry Ford once famously said: "If I had asked my customers what they wanted, they would have told me a faster horse."

By getting to know your customers, understanding their motives, and learning how marketing tactics can influence their decisions, you'll ensure your business or product remains your customers' first choice.

The shortfalls of traditional market research

Traditional consumer research, while it undoubtedly gives companies certain insights into the marketplace, can also be a red herring — steering you off course and away from your original mission. Implement a series of small changes based on the whims of the current marketplace, and over time, you may end up with a product that's appealing to no one.

It's something the Hershey chocolate company found out the hard way. After many years and countless research studies, Hershey went from being the most trusted American chocolate brand to one whose best-selling products contained little or no real chocolate at all. By focusing on research that put cost savings (substituting vegetable oil for real cocoa butter) over the value of flavor, the company effectively lost its compass, and many of its customers felt betrayed.

So, if market research is so unreliable, why are companies still using it to make decisions? The short answer is: the smart ones aren't. Classic techniques such as surveys and polls have limited reach, with the same group of people often giving the same answers.

We think small businesses shouldn't even bother going down the traditional research route. Aside from delivering unreliable results and being prohibitively expensive, these methods rarely give you indepth insight into the minds of your customers.

So, how to begin? Start by talking to family and friends, and by putting yourself in your customers' shoes. When we have new additions to the AdWords sales team at Google, for example, they begin by interacting with customers, creating their own accounts, and experiencing what it's like to be on the other side of the equation. The goal, of course, is to make their customers' experience their own.

We also tell businesses we work with to stick to three essential ideas when it comes to customers:

1. **Listen to them**, but don't change everything you're doing. Find a balance.

2. **Look at the data**, but don't consider it in isolation. The vision you began with is critical to your reputation. It's how your customers know you. Don't lose sight of it.

3. **Be innovative**, but stay off the bandwagon. It's safer to trust your experience then to make a business decision based on a hunch or a wild guess.

Cognitive overload

During the 1990s, advertising agencies touted "breaking through the clutter" as a key objective, meaning that in a crowded media market, you have to either stand out or shout the loudest. In today's market, the clutter in question is an Internet-size monster, resulting in the modern form of paralysis known as cognitive overload.

Simply put, your customers, bombarded with an overwhelming volume of information and options, tune out. We believe one of the main reasons people fail to connect with brand communications is that they wish to avoid cognitive overload. As a marketer, it's an important reminder: To engage your customer, you need to simplify the message.

We often demonstrate the concept using Lego blocks. We give each person 10 colored blocks and one set of instructions to put them together. The first person gets typed instructions, the second gets an audio version, and the third gets the standard manual. Can you guess who finishes the fastest? The standard manual. Why? Because of the three, the standard manual is the only one that presents both pictures and text. To follow the all-type manual, you have to visualize the order and color in your head. To follow the verbal instructions, you have to focus on memorization.

When you design a landing page or a form, or give customers a set of instructions, think carefully about what exactly you want them to do. Ask your friends, family members, and employees to try it first (and don't help them). This will test how truly intuitive the process is. By finding the sweet spot between graphics and text, you'll reduce cognitive overload, see higher conversion rates, and have more grateful customers.

Cognitive lock-in

Cognitive lock-in essentially means that we're creatures of habit. To reduce cognitive overload, we get used to doing things in a certain way, freeing up mental space and leaving room for other things.

Your local supermarket, for instance, is laid out in a certain pattern. If the owners change the layout, you'll likely still go to the aisle where you first found an item, and you may feel mildly annoyed. Supermarkets often see a drop in revenue for several weeks before people's brains adjust to the change.

This insight also applies to acquisition and retention in your business. Your goal should be to keep things familiar and manage change carefully. Don't expect everyone to be as excited about your new website as you are, even if it's clearly improved. You might see the benefits, but make sure your customers see the benefits, too. Point out the changes, and invite feedback so that your customers stay engaged and feel included in the process.

Left-brain and right-brain thinking

We know this is getting into the deep weeds of marketing science here, but we believe it's important if you're going to understand how your customers really think. Of the two brain hemispheres, the left brain is more focused on reasoning, numbers, language, and right-hand control. The right brain is concentrated on imagination, aesthetics, music, and left-hand control. So, are there left-brain and right-brain media channels? We think there are, and as a marketer, it pays to keep them in mind.

Traditionally, direct marketing media (communications that require an immediate response) are processed in the left brain. Visual media such as film and photography are more right-brain functions.

Do you remember the last time you laughed or cried about a piece of direct mail? Exactly. Direct marketing appeals to the more rational side of your brain. But chances are you remember the last time you cried while watching a movie. That's because movies are primarily processed in your right brain, which engages emotions. Both the left and the right brain need to be engaged appropriately to drive maximum response and get your customers to make an effective purchasing decision.

Creative agencies often come up with campaigns that give no thought to how our brains actually work, focusing entirely on a campaign's aesthetics — fast cars, beautiful sunsets, pretty models. When engaging with left-brain media (mailers, coupons, promotional incentives), your customers want specifics. A witty headline and three bullet points will not cut it.

Conversely, if you're using video to sell a product, showing viewers a long list of product benefits is not going to tickle the emotional right brain.

Before your next campaign, you need to ask yourself: Is the medium I'm using aligned with the message I'm giving?

Performance marketing

Our conviction is that as a small business, any marketing you do — product to brand — should be performance marketing. That means every single dollar you spend needs to work and at the very least pay you back one to one. If it doesn't, you haven't figured out a successful marketing strategy.

If you've placed an ad in the Yellow Pages for seven years in a row and aren't sure if it's effective, try a year without it. See if your numbers go down. At the same time, put the money somewhere else, and test that channel, too. It's an easy way to see whether the money you're allotting to your marketing channels is being wasted.

You should also strive for an integrated marketing strategy, often referred to as a 360-degree approach. Basically, you should look in more than one direction, so none of your customers are left out in the cold. For many businesses, that translates to not putting all your eggs in one basket — that is, all digital or all traditional.

At Google, our approach to engagement and performance marketing is to strive for maximum relevance and hyperpersonalization. In a nutshell, we want to keep our customers interested and interacting with our brand using all means available — social, mobile, video, and everything in between.

Our advice is: Don't focus solely on the net response of a single campaign — for example, going from a 1 percent response to a 1.5 percent response. It's a solid achievement, but you need to keep your eye on the big picture, and at the ways your target audience is being engaged overall. If 1 percent responded initially, that's the tip of the proverbial iceberg, with the other 99 percent still below.

A good example of 360-degree marketing comes from the Great Urban Race, a sophisticated urban quest that requires teams to solve clues and complete wacky physical challenges while discovering their city in a brand new way. Founder Joe Reynolds started the business in Chicago with just $5,000. In five years, he and partner Ryan Kunkel have turned his initial investment into Red Frog Events, a company with more than 60 full-time employees and three signature events that take place in more than 35 cities across the United States and Europe, drawing more than 500,000 participants and spectators. Revenue has grown from $50,000 in 2007 to a projected $85 million in 2012.

Reynolds relies heavily on social channels for his marketing, but he also capitalizes on capturing the excitement at the actual events and posting photos and video to generate buzz. His website also provides links to Red Frog's other events, Warrior Dash and the Firefly Music Festival, which in addition to targeting different audiences, offer opportunities for volunteering, sponsorship, charitable giving, and partnership. Using a variety of media and channels, Reynolds found ways to appeal to a broad spectrum of customers, and cover a wide range of age groups and interests.

Whether you're launching your first website, thinking about ways to connect your offline and online channels, or trying to build your brand or customer loyalty, a 360-degree strategy ensures that your marketing dollars will have maximum impact with the largest possible audience.

What's Next?
The future of small business

It's estimated that by 2020, online connection speeds will be 500 times faster in the United States than they are today, with countries such as South Korea reaching those speeds even sooner.[24]

Rather than be intimidated by this prediction, we hope you embrace it and use it your advantage. Taking a cue from sheep farmers in Sardinia, shoe designers in Australia, and ice-cream makers in San Francisco, small businesses everywhere are already finding ways to harness the power of online to grow and thrive in the modern business world.

As we gaze into our crystal ball, we also see consumers demanding, and companies like Google delivering, new ways to get search results faster, more accurately, and with more relevancy, in the way, shape, form, and price they prefer. That, combined with the exponential growth and evolution of mobile devices, will single-handedly change the way consumers behave.

By the end of 2013, the number of mobile devices will exceed the world's population, and more Americans will access the web via mobile than from their desktops.[25]

For anyone who's sat on a commuter train and watched people tapping away on their phones, the implications for society are already apparent. In her State of the Web address, Mary Meeker, a partner in the venture capital firm Kleiner Perkins Caufield

& Byers, projected a 42 percent increase in smartphone subscriptions in 2012, bringing the estimated global total to 1.1 billion users.

The ramifications for small businesses are possibly even more far-reaching. Consider, for instance, that in the last 5,000 years, the way we pay for things has only changed three times: from barter to coin, from coin to paper, and from paper to plastic.

With recent advances in mobile technology, people can now research and pay for products in an entirely new way. Consumers today use maps on their mobile phones to find businesses and perhaps take advantage of an online offer sent to their phone to get a discount.

When they walk into a store, they can compare prices and even pay their parking meters from their mobile devices while browsing the aisles. Finally (and most importantly), they can purchase their products via phone — no cash or credit card required.

In places like San Francisco, some businesses are already eliminating cash payment from the process. Split Bread, an artisan sandwich shop, asks customers to scan barcodes with their smartphones to pull up a digital menu, then order and pay via phone. Other small operators use mobile-payment services such as Google Wallet, PayPal Here, and Square rather than credit cards.

What these developments signify is essentially the unification of offline and online commerce, which we think will revolutionize how people do business. In a Pew Research Center study of the mobile-payment industry, experts went so far as to predict that phones could replace cash and credit cards both online and in stores within a decade.[26]

While human interaction — being able to see and touch the product, talk to an expert about it, and compare it to other products — will continue to be motivators for transactions, more and more consumers will find ways to make the purchase process easier and more efficient.

In the past five years, we have looked at thousands of small businesses and have met with hundreds of entrepreneurs in more than 40 countries around the world. Across the board, we have been hugely inspired and greatly humbled by the creativity, vision, and dedication they have shown.

We know that in today's economy, it is not easy to succeed. But we hope that we have conveyed to you our very strong belief that the opportunity is there for the taking.

In many countries, it is young people who are especially affected by economic challenges. Despite these hurdles, we have met many young entrepreneurs who are actually leading the way in thinking big about the Internet — building very healthy businesses online with nothing more than a laptop, an HD webcam, and a big helping of passion, determination and creativity.

As a result, we're betting on small business to lead the charge in the new global economy. In today's infinite market, the world is literally at your fingertips.

And it all begins with that first digital step.

Acknowledgements

Over the past five years, we have had the unique privilege and pleasure of working with the most amazing colleagues, partners and small businesses around the world.

Their energy, determination and stories form the inspiration for this book. The idea took shape over many late-night conversations, working sessions in planes, and conference calls during holidays.

One key thing we most certainly learned is that it is not easy to write. We hope that the experiences and stories we have chosen to share with you are both interesting and helpful.

Throughout the process, we have had the kind help and inspiration of many people and would like to thank some specifically:

Our summer interns, Carlos Flores Rodriguez and Rishi Shah, were a huge help in selecting the right stories and examples. Our colleague, Victoria Tchoudakov, gave us the benefit of her keen eye for structure and logic.

As we're both non-native speakers, the book would not have read this easily and well without the help of Bonnie Wach, Benjamin Roy and Kelly Littlejohn.

We would also like to thank our employer, Google, and specifically Lorraine Twohill and Jen Fitzpatrick, for all the support.

Google has given us the opportunity to find these stories, make a real difference, and also make friends for life. "Working on important things that matter in the world" (to quote our founders Larry and Sergey) is a mantra we take to work and to heart every day.

Last but not least, we want to thank all the small businesses around the globe that have shared their stories with us and with the world. They are a true inspiration for all of us.

Arjan Dijk and Sandeep Menon
May 2013

Notes

1. Google, "B2B Pulse Check Report," 2010.

2. U.S. Small Business Administration, "Advocacy Small Business Statistics and Research," http://web.sba.gov.

3. Joan Ganz Cooney Center / Sesame Workshop, "Always Connected: The New Digital Media Habits of Young Children" (March 20, 2011), http://www.joanganzcooneycenter.org/publication/always-connected-the-new-digital-media-habits-of-young-children/.

4. BusinessWire, "Research Now for AVG" (October 2010), http://www.businesswire.com/news/home/20101006006722/en/Digital-Birth-Online-World.

5. Mary Meeker, Kleiner Perkins Caufield Byers, "State of the Web / Internet Trends" (2012), PCB / International Telecommunications Union.

6. Cisco® Visual Networking Index (VNI) Global Mobile Data Traffic Forecast, 2011 to 2016, http://www.cisco.com/en/US/solutions/collateral/ ns341/ns525/ns537/ns705/ns827/white_paper_c11-520862.html.

7. ComScore, "Google Reaches 1 Billion Global Visitors" June 2011, http://www.comscoredatamine.com/2011/06/google-reaches-1-billion-global-visitors/.

8. Google, "B2B Pulse Check Report," 2010.

9. Google, "Online Savviness & Activity Among Small Business Owners" (March 2010).

10. McKinsey Global Institute, "Internet Matters: The Net's Sweeping Impact on Growth, Jobs, and Prosperity" (May 2011), http://www.mckinsey.com/insights/mgi/research/technology_and_inno vation/internet_matters.

11. Google Local Search Usage Study, "Bridging the Caps, From Search to Sales" (August 2012).

12. Peterson Institute for International Economics, 2011.

13. Jim Lecinski, *ZMOT: Winning the Zero Moment of Truth*, Google eBooks, 2012.

14. Bazaarvoice, 2010–2012, http://www.bazaarvoice.com/social-commerce-statistics.

15. Brad Smallwood, Head of Measurement and Insights, Facebook (October 1, 2012), http://www.facebook-studio.com/news/item/making-digital-brand-campaigns-better.

16. "State Bicycle: Building a Strong Customer Base," www.facebook.com/advertising/success-stories/state-bicycle.

17. The Journal.ie, "I put my family business on Facebook. Here's what happened" (May 19, 2012), http://www.thejournal.ie/readme/column-i-put-my-family-business-on-facebook-here%E2%80%99s-what-happened/.

18. Patagonia, "Our History," http://www.patagonia.com/us/patagonia.go?&assetid=3351.

19. Hada Gold, "Brazen Life" (March 9, 2012), http://blog.brazencareerist.com/2012/03/09/secrets-exposed-how-did-you-turn-your-cooking-blog-into-a-full-time-job/.

20. Meaghan Haire, "A Brief History of the Walkman," *Time*, July 1, 2009, http://www.time.com/time/nation/article/0,8599,1907884,00.html#ixz z292UzAaoH.

21 Eric Markowitz, "Three Reasons Warby Parker Is Killing It," *Inc.*, March 7, 2012, http://www.inc.com/eric-markowitz/3-reasons-warby-parker-is-killing-it.html?nav=next.

22. Yahoo, "Flickr – Advertising Solution," http://advertising.yahoo.com/article/flickr.html.

23. 31 Stories of Small Business Success, Inc., "Making Life Easier for his Customers," May 9, 2011, http://www.inc.com/articles/201105/small-business-success-stories-zanes-cycles.html.

24. Jim Lecinski, *ZMOT: Winning the Zero Moment of Truth*, Google eBooks, 2012.

25. Cisco Visual Networking Index, *Global Mobile Data Traffic Forecast*, February 6, 2013.

26. Aaron Smith, Janna Anderson, and Lee Rainie, "The Future of Money in a Mobile Age" (April 17, 2012), http://www.pewinternet.org/Reports/2012/Future-of-Money.aspx.

20737200R00055

Made in the USA
Charleston, SC
26 July 2013Made in the USA
Charleston, SC
26 July 2013